I0126490

Beautiful Life

Beautiful Life

Edited by
Amanda Brohier
and
Robyn Graham

Connor Court Publishing

Published in 2019 by Connor Court Publishing Pty Ltd
Copyright © Amanda Brohier and Robyn Graham, 2019

All rights reserved. No part of this book may be reproduced or transmitted in any form or by any means, electronic or mechanical, including photocopying, recording or by any information storage and retrieval system, without prior permission in writing from the publisher.

Connor Court Publishing Pty Ltd
PO Box 7257
Redland Bay QLD 4165

sales@connorcourt.com
www.connorcourtpublishing.com.au
Phone 0497 900 685

ISBN: 9781925826746

Front Cover Photo: ISTOCKPHOTO
Front Cover Design: Maria Giordano
Printed in Australia

Contents

Foreword

I am honoured to write the foreword to this book, '*Beautiful Life*'. Dedicated to telling the true stories of women who found themselves with a crisis pregnancy, they reveal to us the personal circumstances that led each woman to considering abortion. In doing so, we are given great insights into how the lie that choosing abortion is empowering for her is firmly embedded in our culture, and how effectively it has been in silencing those around her. By instilling fear in them, it leaves her with very little strength to resist the pull towards abortion as being the only real solution.

As a pro-life medical lawyer, I feel sad for the way in which abortion law reform has occurred, and the terrible precedent it sets for the discussion of any serious issue that involves deep moral questions. Even with outliers ready to put their reputations and livelihood on the line, very little attention is given to the pursuit of truth when it comes to abortion. The inability to guarantee that contraceptive drugs and devices can separate sex from the transmission of human life means that abortion is accepted by many as necessary for a modern society. But now we have to deal with our guilt.

Legalising abortion as standard healthcare can make society feel less guilty about their personal experience with abortion, as the woman who has undergone abortion, or her partner and the father of the child, or as friends and family of the woman who stood back to let her make her own decision, and supported her through its aftermath. We have to deal with the fact we might have left her on her own, and did not offer her our real opinion for fear of being socially uncomfortable and offending her. Instead, we just told her to try and forget about it, and move forward with life.

Nature, however, presents a powerful counterpoint argument. Whilst pregnancy and the seemingly insurmountable challenges it brings may be erased through abortion, the physical and mental sequelae will manifest notwithstanding this. Physically, her body never forgets that at one point in time, there was a human life growing inside her. She must disclose this fact as part of her medical history. Mentally, the fracturing of her dignity as a woman can be too much to deal with, so she may numb herself as a form of self-protection, or become as one woman puts it, "as hard as granite".

We trust our lawmakers to lead on important issues. In Australia, abortion law reform has transformed abortion from being a principled exception in our criminal law, where it was left to the doctor to decide whether her life or health was at grave risk of harm, to a standard health service that can be requested for any reason. The embedding of the ideology in the law that the ability to choose is good for the community impacts the morality of the community. As one woman in the book puts it, "I told myself that abortion was legal therefore it couldn't be as bad as I thought."

A strong theme of this book is the lack of honest information imparted by health care providers to women on what abortion is, and the development of the unborn child, and the lack of referral to crisis pregnancy services oriented towards helping the woman find the strength and support to continue on with pregnancy for her own good, and for the good of the unborn child. In what seems like an overwhelming number of cases, the act of abortion was not freely chosen by her.

Advocates for choice decry the need for such services, claiming they peddle in misinformation and seek to shame women. On the one hand they say abortion is a difficult decision, yet they say giving her information on what she is about to do, or the support available that could assist her to continue pregnancy, will cause her greater harm than the abortion. It is an interesting argument, only because despite being devoid of all logic, it has been sold in the market place of ideas, and accepted by sophisticated people blinded by the power to control human reproduction.

Another strong theme of this book is the phenomenon of abortion coercion, whereby a woman undergoes abortion as the result of undue influence by a partner, sometimes involving threats of violence, or the threat of being abandoned. Acknowledged to be a real phenomenon by abortion clinic operators, the response of the medical profession to developing a policy for screening for it, has been slow. Many abortions take place in private clinics, where there is a clear conflict of interest in them providing in-house counselling, which highlights the complexity of abortion as a "free choice."

The notorious "safe access zone laws" that operate in most parts of Australia are a legal embarrassment. They prevent side walk counsellors outside abortion clinics from conveying information to women who are willing to hear about the alternatives to abortion. In many cases, states have suppressed free speech, and elevated discussion about abortion taking place within an enormous area around a clinic to be a criminal offence. Under these safe access zone laws, side walk counsellors are a menace. Their mere presence is threatening to a woman's safety and dignity.

In my home state of New South Wales, sidewalk counsellors are a bona fide health hazard regulated under the *Public Health Act*. This is despite the fact that there is no reliable evidence that their activities have ever harmed women more than the abortion she subsequently underwent, and much anecdotal evidence that they have helped many women choose not to abort. We all know that the truth can hurt, but it can also be the inspiration for noble actions. However our society rejects the notion of objective truth, and as a result, the pro-abortion ideology flourishes.

With abortion on demand the common legal position in Australia, you might be tempted to believe there is little hope, but I believe there is. People are waking up and understand they must stand up and be counted on this threshold issue. Whilst we have not yet reached the stage where abortion is forced on women, we can still say "No!" and support pregnant women through privately funded crisis pregnancy centres, support the community through education initiatives, and support our leaders who have the courage to say that abortion is the taking of human life.

This book will bring tears to your eyes and challenge any misconceptions you may have had about how a woman can allow herself to be pressured into undergoing abortion, and how the unique trauma of that decision can impact her life and those around her forever. The importance of this wonderful book cannot be overstated. I commend it to any person who seeks the truth about abortion. Whilst it is important for all people to read this book, I particularly commend it to health professionals so they are empowered to refuse to participate in this grotesque parody of healthcare.

Anna Walsh

Lawyer/Academic

University of Notre Dame, Sydney

PhD Candidate (UNDA), M. Bioethics (Harvard), LLM (res) (Syd), LLB (Hons),

B Nurs (Hons), Grad Dip. Leg. Prac.

2 September 2019

Preface

This collection of intimate and very personal experiences that you hold in your hand contains fourteen real life Australian stories about abortion. The aim of this collection is to give a voice to women who have experienced abortion first hand and enable them to share about their very real world experiences and the subsequent impact of the abortion on their lives.

The experiences of each woman, while containing overlapping themes, identify some common and profound personal concerns which need to be addressed.

They include:

- Abortion coercion exists for women at their most vulnerable and needs to be exposed and addressed so that all women can make considered and not coerced choices.

- Pre-abortion counselling must include all options for women, including opportunities to receive support for those who wish to continue their pregnancy.

- Post abortion grief is a reality and needs to be acknowledged and addressed in pre-abortion counselling.

Researcher and Founding Director of Adelaide Centre for Bioethics and Culture in Australia, Dr. Greg Pike, in his paper on Abortion and Women's Health, highlights the complexity of the decision to have an abortion. He correctly identifies that, "Deciding to have an abortion

is far more complex than simply not intending to become pregnant".[1]
He further states that, "Women rarely see babies themselves as a
threat, and instead feel positively towards them. However, it is the
related experiences, like the future stress and difficulty of parenthood,
financial stress, loss of freedom, ongoing violence or deprivation that
women may be hoping to avoid by seeking abortion."[2]

The stories in this book illustrate the reality of these concerns
in women's lives and sadly also illustrate that in most cases these
concerns were not addressed in any pre-abortion counselling. It is
therefore our desire in publishing these experiences to highlight the
needs of women who find themselves facing an unplanned pregnancy
so that we as a society can put in place better support services for
those in this crucial decision making stage and those post abortion
women who need support and healing.

We are profoundly indebted to these brave women who have been
willing to speak about their experience and dedicate this book to them
and indeed to all women who have been through, are facing or will
face similar experiences. While minor changes have been made to the
stories we have endeavoured to edit the stories as little as possible so
that the voice you hear will be that of the women themselves.

Amanda Brohier (B.Sc., Dip. Nutr & Diet)
Robyn Graham (former RN & RM)
August 2019

---

[1]   Pike, G (2017) Abortion and Women's Health https://www.spuc.org.uk/pub-
lications-library/750-abortion-and-womens-health-april-2017-pdf/file accessed 13 August 2019
[2]   Ibid

Coercion

The Oxford dictionary defines coercion as, "The action or practice of persuading someone to do something by using force or threats". The United Nations Committee on the Elimination of Discrimination against Women (CEDAW) have identified that, "violations of women's sexual and reproductive health rights are frequent. These take many forms including ... performance of procedures related to women's reproductive and sexual health without the woman's consent, including ... forced abortion."[3]

While the following stories do not illustrate abortion by physical force, they demonstrate that emotional coercion to abort in response to threats is very real for some women. Women who were persuaded to discontinue their pregnancy by their partner or husband against their will were submitted to threats ranging from, "it will ruin my life" and "I will leave you" to "it's not the right time in my career" and "we can't afford it". Others said that, "My husband told me that he wasn't interested and to get rid of it... Even more, if I didn't, I would have to leave." Some stories illustrate the emotional turmoil that some women face. Sonya says that, "My heart wanted to keep the baby, my head said no. In short, my boyfriend didn't want a child so my head won and we aborted." Julie submitted to her husband's career goals, "No baby would interfere with the master plan he had for his life."

One scientific study identifies the importance of the partner's attitude in decision making. The authors identified that, "Some women were exposed to pressure from their partners to have an abortion and asked themselves whether it was right to have a child that

---

3   United Nations Office of the High Commissioner on Human Rights. Sexual and reproductive health and rights https://www.ohchr.org/EN/Issues/Women/WRGS/Pages/HealthRights.aspx accessed 14 August 2019

might threaten their relationship as a couple. One woman described it like this: "I have thought I have to have an abortion, as he is afraid our relationship will end if we have a child."[4]

In a recent article in The Australian, Rachel Wong identifies that, "Recent polls in NSW and Queensland show that one in four people knows at least one woman who has been pressured into having an abortion. In 2017, NSW saw two shocking cases of NRL players who had coerced their girlfriends into having abortions. Last year, during parliamentary hearings on the Queensland abortion bill, an abortion provider admitted to performing abortions on women she knew were being coerced. How's that for pro-"choice"?[5]

The evidence Wong was probably referring to was that of Dr Carol Portman, one of Queensland's only later term abortion providers. While speaking at a Committee Hearing for the *Termination of Pregnancy Bill* Portman said, "Sometimes even in the best of circumstances we understand that a person is to a degree being coerced but feel they still need to go ahead ... because it's their only choice, because otherwise this person will leave them, and their 4 kids (for example). It's very hard to know what to do in those circs so you go ahead with what their choice is even though to a degree they are being coerced."[6] Dr. Portman's evidence sheds light on the pressures that some women are under when they face the decision of whether to terminate or not. Coerced consent is not consent.

Of great concern are the results from one study that identified that, "women who experienced coercion or pressure and lack of

---

[4]   Kjelsvik et al. (2018)Women's experiences when unsure about whether or not to have an abortion in the first trimester https://www.tandfonline.com/action/showCitFormats?doi=10.1080%2F07399332.2018.1465945 accessed 14 August 2019

[5]   Wong, R. (2019) Abortion won't stop violence, The Advertiser, Adelaide, 8 August, 2019

[6]   Real Choices Australia http://realchoices.org.au/2018/09/abortion-coercion-admitted accessed 14 August 2019.

support when considering an abortion or those who had a history of psychiatric illness, were at greater risk for developing mental health problems after the abortion.[7]

In a social environment where women's rights are being championed more than ever before, Rachel Wong's question is thus pertinent. How is this pro-choice? A further question then needs to be addressed. How can this situation be remedied?

One answer surely must be to address the issue of adequate provision of health care in relation to professional counselling. In Jaya's story there are obvious flaws in the provision of adequate counselling. She said that, "I did have hope, however. I knew that the clinic might deny the procedure if it seemed I wasn't happy to go ahead... The counsellor asked why I was aborting and I told her we had only known each other for four months. She replied that that was a valid reason to have an abortion. That was it."

Jaya's story is verified by others who report that they felt there was no option for them. In an article on "Women's experiences when unsure about whether or not to have an abortion in the first trimester," the authors identify that, "the feeling of shame at being caught in an unplanned pregnancy and considering termination could be a hindrance for presenting for the need for counselling. As a married woman, a client, said: 'I think you are so vulnerable that you cannot make yourself do it [ask to have a talk about doubt].'"[8]

In any other medical situation, a practitioner is obliged to present all options to their patient and ensure that the patient is fully aware of any risks should the patient decide to proceed. In the same way, a skilled

---

[7]   Broen, A.N., Moum, T., Bodtker, A.S. and Ekeberg, O. (2005) The course of mental health after miscarriage and induced abortion: a longitudinal, five-year follow-up study. BMC Medicine, 3(18), 14pp.

[8]   Kjelsvik et al. (2018)Women's experiences when unsure about whether or not to have an abortion in the first trimester

counsellor will ensure that the client is aware of all options available to them before making a decision. Such a life changing decision as an abortion should not be made during a short interview with no opportunity to discuss options available as occurred in Jaya's story. Madeleine's story illustrates a further issue of inadequate counselling where blatant misinformation was given.

In the magazine, *the American Feminist*, Marion Syversen says that, "One-sided information ... leads to bad decisions... So many women are pressured or coerced into abortion, either told outright to have one—like I was—or given no support to do anything else. People who talk to women facing unplanned pregnancies must realize that they are standing on thin ice. They need to be careful, weigh their words with respect, and give information while recognizing that they could be changing the course of a woman's whole life. What will she do if she's only given one choice? How long will it take for her to recover?"[9]

In her book, *"Fearfully and Wonderfully Made"*, Dr. Megan Best quotes from a 1995 Australian research project to identify women's considerations while deciding to have an abortion. She concludes that, "It is obvious that lack of support, lack of confidence and coercion play an important part in the choice to abort."[10] Adequate provision of support mechanisms and supportive counselling are thus key to enabling women to overcome coercion and thus truly have genuine choice.

[9]   The American Feminist. Fall/Winter 2011 pp. 33 https://www.feministsforlife.org/wp accessed 14 August

[10]   Best, M. Fearfully and Wonderfully Made, Matthias Media, Kingsford, NSW, 2012. pp:182-183

Jaya's Story

I'll never forget the day. My period was late so I thought I'd do a pregnancy test to confirm I wasn't pregnant so I wouldn't stress about it and possibly delay my period further. I was expecting it to be negative. I put it down expecting the one line and as I went to throw it away, I realised there were double lines. I was shocked, but I also remember in that moment, I was excited. In seconds I went from me, myself and I, to knowing I was sharing my body with someone else.

As my boyfriend had an important meeting that day, I thought I'd wait until that evening to tell him. I told my mum who wasn't very happy. I was a single mother and she was concerned about the situation. We had only been seeing each other for four months. Whilst I was fully aware the pregnancy was ill timed, I was still a little bit excited overall.

It was hours before I was able to tell my boyfriend and I was nervous. I had semi-scripted in my head how the conversation would go; we would both be shocked that this was happening but ultimately we would have to step up to the responsibility and would be welcoming a baby.

Coercion

What happened was the last thing that I expected.

"I'm pregnant," I said.

"I knew you were going to say that," he replied, "but we are having an abortion." I was completely thrown. He knew I was almost coerced into aborting my young daughter so I was dumbfounded.

"There is no way we are having a baby," he kept saying. I became extremely defensive and told him that I would raise the baby on my own and not to worry about it.

I received a text message saying that he was sorry for his reaction and that he had never cried so much in his life but knowing that he had a kid running around would haunt him for the rest of his life. In my mind, he was saying, "Enjoy being a single mum but it makes me feel sick that you would keep the baby."

On the day I found out I was pregnant I was distraught, confused, hurt and frustrated. I already had a daughter to a relationship where I was not in contact with her father so the thought of being a woman with two kids to two different fathers who were both absent was incredibly daunting and devastating. What I cared about most was what others would think. I was so embarrassed.

The next days were a blur but what was worst was the clear message - if you want to be with me, get rid of the baby. If you keep the baby, I'm gone. I felt torn because I really cared for this man and he kept telling me that this baby would ruin his life. I didn't want to do that to him or lose him. At the same time I was concerned that having an abortion would ruin mine, and I would be full of regret.

A few days later, morning sickness hit and I was experiencing extreme illness. I couldn't keep food down and I struggled to sleep. I had to tell my boss about what was going on and she agreed that an abortion would be a better option. The three people to whom I was closest weren't happy about my pregnancy.

A few days after that I went to the toilet and a huge gush of blood came out. Could it be I was having a miscarriage? I was upset but somewhat relieved. Perhaps the decision was going to be taken out of my hands. I decided to pray for a miscarriage. I had already experienced a miscarriage before so I thought it best to go to a doctor. My boyfriend came with me and I had a plan. I would get an ultrasound and he would feel empathy and realise it was a human being. However, the whole time we were at the doctors he complained about wanting to go home, that it was taking too long and was then disappointed to hear it was nothing and the pregnancy was going strong.

More Pressure

The situation continued. I was defending the pregnancy and he was pressuring me into having an abortion. I then sent him a text message saying that I couldn't do this anymore and that I didn't want to have an abortion. I said that it was sending me crazy feeling that he was forcing me to have one and that I couldn't do it even though he said I have to raise it on my own and that I would lose my career and probably my house. I told him it wasn't fair that he was just going to walk away from me because this wasn't convenient for him. If my option was to have it on my own, then fine, but he could walk away and let me get on with my life. I received no reply.

The truth is I was hoping he would step up and I kept faith that he would but my fear of him hating me and that I was ruining his life continually played on my mind. I decided to contact him days later and talk about terminating the pregnancy and he replied. I realise now I was so emotionally manipulated into believing I needed him, that I was willing to compromise my values just to have him in my life. As the weeks went on and the sicker and more exhausted I became, the decision to abort was made out of defeat. I gave up. I gave in. And perhaps I wouldn't regret it. Everyone else seemed so blasé about it so I wasn't even sure why I was making such a big deal of it.

I booked in for a termination. The people closest to me were aware this was happening and that I wanted to keep the baby but no one stepped in. We took the train and arrived at the clinic. I was sad to be there but was too scared to say so. I've always been a people pleaser so I worried that I had made such a fuss about going there and that he would be mad at me if I brought up my concerns again.

Poor Counselling

I did have hope, however. I knew that the clinic might deny the procedure if it seemed I wasn't happy to go ahead so I filled the forms out to get ready for my pre-abortion consultation with a "professional therapist". The counsellor asked why I was aborting and I told her we had only known each other for four months. She replied that that was a valid reason to have an abortion. That was it.

I was officially defeated. I was making a huge deal out of this; I was being a drama queen. I was being difficult and I was inconveniencing everyone including my workplace because of how sick I was. No one cared about me or was bothered this was a baby. No one loved the baby so I agreed to it. I just wanted it to be over.

As I entered the surgery, it was loud, cold and the atmosphere felt hostile. As they were about to administer the anaesthetic I wanted to leave. I wanted to say no and walk out but I was too scared to leave still being pregnant. The last thing I remember was the ceiling becoming like a wave and I woke up in a recliner chair next to the girl who was crying hysterically in the waiting room earlier that morning. As I regained consciousness, my partner had been called to pick me up but he was running late. I wanted another drink but felt too scared to ask because the nurse looked frustrated that I was still sitting there. In the end I was asked to leave and wait outside. Ten minutes later my boyfriend arrived.

The next day I went to work and I actually felt good. I had no sickness, I was relieved that there was nothing to fight about and I had energy and vitality. My boyfriend decided to go out with his friends saying that he deserved it because of how stressed he had been. I agreed with him. The next day was my daughter's fifth birthday party so I spent the day surrounded by family and friends and felt relatively good.

However, the next day I remember waking up and feeling like I was hit by a truck, both physically and emotionally. The regret started to set in and I was able to think clearly for the first time in weeks. I was so frustrated with myself and full of anger. I quit my job that day and stormed out of my workplace, never to return. I called my boyfriend to tell him I wanted to talk about the abortion only to be told that he didn't want to bring up the past and that I was just fishing for an argument. I was beside myself that I had allowed the abortion and started thinking of how to make this right again. I was in damage control.

As the months went on, my relationship became extremely toxic and abusive. I was struggling to not think of the pregnancy but it was all consuming. I was obsessed by it. At first I masked my pain by partying, drinking and gambling. In the meantime, I also tried to get pregnant again so I could fix my mistake. I would lie that I was on contraception in the hope of conceiving again.

Depression and Anxiety

I was unaware that I was suffering from depression and anxiety and started to normalise behaviours such as not eating, not leaving the house, wanting to isolate myself through the week then trying to party on the weekends. I was crying all day and night and allowing myself to be treated horribly by my boyfriend while struggling to be a good mother. I could barely smile and I'd have awful thoughts about ending my life. As I became a shell of myself I suppose I became less attractive and my boyfriend started to distance himself from me, making me extremely clingy and anxious about being left alone and left by him. He had told me he would leave me if I had the baby but even though I had the termination he still left me. I was furious.

Gaslighted and Suicidal

I was so angry and devastated and felt that I was unworthy of life. Death seemed the best way to take the pain away. One night I made plans to throw myself in front of a train. Knowing my daughter needed me was the only thing that kept me here. I became so mentally unwell that I had a complete breakdown. I had endured months of an abusive relationship where I was coerced into an abortion and then gaslighted into believing I was worthless. I was fading fast.

Abortion Grief

I can't tell you how it happened but as I sat ready to leave the state and drive away from my life, the two words "abortion grief" popped into my head and a voice told me to google them. There it was - the validation I so desperately needed. I wasn't insane, I was possibly suffering from Post-Traumatic Stress Disorder (PTSD) from the abortion and the effects listed were everything I was going through. I felt hopeful for the first time in a long time. I could get the much needed help I was desperate for. Abortion is seen as one of those things that I should be grateful to have access to, so I didn't think I could feel sadness about it because it was "my choice" and I should have been grateful for the choice. But this was not my choice.

A few months earlier my friend had posted about a counselling service that offers free counselling to those who have had an abortion or are in challenging pregnancies so I decided to email them. They called me straight away and I remember thinking how caring they were and I felt important which felt nice. I walked into my first counselling session and for the first time I was told that what I went through was not ok.

Anne's Story

Having had two abortions myself is a pain, regret and loss that I will live with forever. The two abortions I had some 14 years ago should never have been allowed to happen. Sadly, I was not only encouraged to have them; I was also told it was not a baby but just a blob of lifeless cells that wouldn't be viable anyway.

I am compelled to share my story with you, in the hope that it educates women who find themselves where I found myself and worst of all surrounded by all the wrong people and apparent professionals telling me it was ok, it wasn't wrong, all sorts of people did it, it's the best choice you have, you will never look back, there is no baby therefore it won't feel anything and this will not be a viable pregnancy.

On both occasions I didn't want to go through with the abortion but very sadly and unfortunately I did. Both times the "procedure" was not "successful" so I was rushed back into theatre to have emergency procedures to complete the procedure "properly" again. I can't even begin to explain the feeling of complete emptiness and absolute loss compounded by being in the maternity ward full of new mums with their newborns.

I remember so clearly being held down and not wanting to go ahead with the abortion and being told that I didn't have a choice now. I also remember my body so desperately not wanting to let go of what my spirit and soul knew and recognised as life. I can't go back and change the past but I can choose to always make educated, moral and honourable choices.

I later experienced three miscarriages. The losses of these babies are also a loss I live with forever. I have named the five babies that are in heaven and I look forward to the day that we are all reunited.

I have six beautiful children, and a sponsor child who lives in Africa for whom I am so grateful. A total of 12 children.

I become a Christian around six years ago and I believe I have been forgiven, restored and made whole again. I am now a disciple of Christ.

The truth really does set you free. I wish someone had told me the truth back then.

Polly's Story[11]

I didn't have a happy childhood at all. I always felt very isolated and very sad. By the time puberty hit I was desperate for someone to love me. I discovered boys and sex. I left school at 15 to do hairdressing and life just cruised along. I used to drink a lot and I slept around, desperate for love.

When I was 20, I was married to a man that I didn't love. I didn't know what a loving home was until his family loved me so I married into their love. I had always wanted to be a mother and he had a brother 13 years his junior that I spent a lot of time caring for as his mother had poor health.

Coerced to Abort

Not long after we got married I became pregnant. My husband told me that he wasn't interested and to get rid of it. Just like that. Even more, if I didn't, I would have to leave. I think I cried nearly nonstop for three weeks. When he asked me after three weeks what I was actually crying about, I made the decision that to stay married, I needed to do as he asked.

After my abortion, my response was overwhelming. I didn't know at the time that what I was experiencing was grief but it was almost all consuming. The feeling of isolation was terrible. How can you talk to someone about what you have done and how much it hurts when you feel so ashamed and after all it was "your choice"?

---

[11] Name changed to preserve anonymity

I felt there would be no-one who would be sympathetic to me so I had to absorb the pain and keep quiet. I started to drink very heavily and when my husband suggested that I would soon become an alcoholic, I agreed and switched to smoking marijuana. I remember one day after a long crying session that I felt 99 years old and there was nothing left to look forward to or live for. All my hopes and dreams felt shattered and I loathed myself. My husband had pressured me to have the abortion, I couldn't forgive him or live with him anymore and I left soon after. I was 22.

Second Abortion

Once you do something such as having an abortion, your heart can become seared. A couple of years later I was living with someone else and conceived again. I was not in the relationship for the long term and didn't want this man in my life forever so I had that baby aborted too. I never gave a thought how he would feel about that.

My heart was now hard as granite. I hated myself and didn't really like anyone else either. Drugs and alcohol were the things that kept me afloat and functioning. There was no shortage of men but I despised them all.

At 25 I had the opportunity to travel through Africa for six months with a friend. On that trip I met an Englishman who loved smoking drugs as much as I did and we became a couple. We got stoned and laughed and laughed, something that I could not ever remember doing before. I told him at one stage that I was not interested in love so not to fall in love with me, I just wanted to have fun!

Before I left Africa he asked me to marry him but I laughed and thought it was just a holiday romance. I cried as I left him in Africa. I felt that I had truly been happy and loved for the first time in my life. He followed me home and continued to pursue me. I told him that he was crazy, that I would be a terrible wife and he would be sorry. When he finally coaxed me into signing the papers I told him not to come crying to me when he was sick of me. We married in front of two witnesses. He was either brave or stupid. By the time I was 26 we were on the dole, travelling in a Kombi van, living in forests and on beaches, smoking marijuana all day every day. Life wasn't always a laugh by then, but we were "searching for something meaningful".

Then disaster struck. My biological clock had been ticking and I decided that I wanted to have a baby, of all things in that situation! Well, with the thought of having a baby, all the things that I had been anesthetising and paralysing with drugs for so long suddenly became awake. All the guilt, all the shame. What right did I have to think God would give me a child?

Psychotic Episode

The short story is that I ended up in the psychiatric ward in Cairns hospital, in a padded cell. I had been brought in by the police because I had "lost touch with reality" and was doing very mad things around Cairns Harbour. I had given my guy the slip. I had exhausted him as I had been quite mad for days and hadn't eaten, slept or stayed still!

One of the things that I did during my madness was to baptize myself in the harbour. I knew that aborting my babies was making me crazy and I believed that only God could forgive me and save me from myself and wash me clean and I desperately wanted that. My guy finally found me and gave them permission to sedate me. After I had slept I had come back to myself and I was taken "home" to the Kombi.

That wasn't the end of my inner turmoil. I could not get any peace now that I was facing my grief and "Pandora's Box" was open. A couple of weeks later I went mad again. The overwhelming guilt was insurmountable. I remember being distraught because there were no markers or monuments to show that my children had ever lived. I had not honoured or remembered them in any way. I felt that death would be too good for me. Then of course I couldn't sleep because I thought I would die.

A few days before this my guy had gone back to Adelaide to get his teeth fixed at the dental hospital. I took a crazy plane journey down to Adelaide while I was still quite mad and still unable to sleep. With my guy's help, I was taken to the home of a lovely man and his wife. This man spoke words of love to me and it seemed like God Himself was talking to me. I stayed there for three days and three nights.

When my guy and I left that home we began brand new lives, full of love. It was miraculous. Nothing was the same. Nothing looked the same. The scales were taken from our eyes and we could see the very thing we had been looking for. We never smoked drugs again. I was loved and forgiven. One year and a week later I held my son in my arms and marvelled at the escape from the hell I had found. I thank God for that.

Life didn't automatically become "beer and skittles". There was a lot of repairing needed in my life and heart and soul. But I was now in the hands of a loving God who gently and patiently peeled back the layers of decay and poured His healing balm into the wounds. I had quite a lot of prayer ministry over the years and He gently gave back the years the "locusts and the canker worms" had eaten.

We now have three living sons and another daughter whom I believe I will meet one day in heaven when I will also meet my first two children. When I look back and see what my abortions did to me, I see a life that was destroyed, actually three lives, first the two babies and then mine. I bought the lie that the baby was a scrap of cells and it would be an easy and convenient solution to a problem. Oh how wrong that is!

Helen's Story

It was a perfect late summer's evening in London where we were currently residing. Good friends of many years' acquaintance from Sydney were visiting. I initially met Julie at the preparatory school gates that our sons attended and the friendships had grown to include husbands and family.

My daughter, Susan, was staying with us with her two-month-old son, Toby. He had woken and she was bringing him out to meet the visitors. On the way, Susie stopped in the kitchen to warm a bottle for Toby. Julie was unable to wait to see the new arrival and she and I went into the kitchen. Our husbands were out on the terrace and well out of earshot.

Julie asked to hold Toby and suddenly, unbelievably, burst into violent floods of tears. Susan and I were totally at a loss to know what could possibly be the matter. I had known Julie for years and had *never* seen her in such a state, nor could I imagine that this beautiful, successful mother of two grown children would be capable of such unrestrained grief!

Julie managed to regain her composure after a few minutes and, realising that she owed us some explanation, went on to explain.

She met her husband, Grant, an ambitious young architect, and they fell head over heels in love and married. Soon after, Julie was pregnant and thoroughly delighted and excited about becoming a mother. She told her husband and the bottom fell out of her world.

Coercion

Grant was ambitious! He wanted to travel…Europe, Britain, the Americas…to look at the greatest architecture the world could offer. Also, raising a family required a home and finance for the inevitable school fees and so on. They must become established first and that was that! No baby would interfere with the master plan he had for his life.

Julie had an abortion. Two and a half years later, there was another.

Eventually when the conditions were favourable, Julie went on to have a son and then a daughter. But she explained that nothing, over two decades, had ever diminished the loss and grief that had wounded her heart forever! She explained that the memories of those two terminated babies never faded and will haunt her for the rest of her life.

Grief

The following six stories have been grouped under the chapter heading, "Grief". However, it can be seen that the stories of the previous chapter also illustrate this consequence of abortion as an ongoing reality for many women. Perhaps the heading would more accurately be the broader term, psychological effects of abortion. Many scientific studies have attempted to definitively measure the psychological effect of abortion on women's health. Studies have come to both positive and negative conclusions. Our book does not attempt to be another literature review on this topic but simply to present the stories as they have been told to us. It may be helpful, however, to comment on some of the extensive work that has already been published.

A review by Bellieni and Buonocore in 2013 in the journal of Psychiatry and Clinical Neurosciences[12] concluded that abortion is linked to adverse mental health outcomes including depression, anxiety disorders (eg: post-traumatic stress disorder) and substance abuse. They concluded that foetal loss exposed women to a higher risk of mental disorders than childbirth.

Another study which is less conclusive is a Norwegian study carried out in 2005 on the effects of abortion and miscarriage on mental health after a five-year period (Broen, Moum, Bodtker and Ekeberg, 2005).[13] This study included 120 women between the ages of 18 and 45. 80 had had an abortion and 40 had experienced a miscarriage.

[12]   Bellieni CV & Buonocore G (2013) Abortion and subsequent mental health: Review of the literature. Psychiatry and Clinical Neurosciences 67:301-310.
[13]   Broen, A.N., Moum, T., Bodtker, A.S. and Ekeberg, O. (2005) The course of mental health after miscarriage and induced abortion: a longitudinal, five-year follow-up study. BMC Medicine, 3(18), 14pp.

According to the authors, the results showed that women who suffered a miscarriage had more "mental distress" ten days following the event and at six months following; however, they showed quicker improvement than women who had experienced an abortion. The authors point out that the women who had miscarriages showed expected responses to a traumatic and sad event. However, the women who had experienced abortion had what they described as "more atypical responses" with elevated scores for guilt, shame and IES (Impact of Event Scale). They believe these findings suggest that the feelings of guilt and shame associated with abortion may contribute to slower improvement in mental health. The authors recommended that women in both groups should be given information concerning possible psychological reactions that women often experience in their situation and they also recommended that follow-up talks should be offered to women.

Dr. Greg Pike, categorises studies on the psychological effects of abortion under the headings of emotional distress, depression and anxiety, post-traumatic stress, substance abuse and self-harm, mental health during a subsequent pregnancy and other disorders including bipolar disorder, neurotic depression and schizophrenic disorders.[14]

Specific mental health issues identified in Dr. Pike's review include a higher risk of psychiatric admission compared with women who carried to term. Adverse mental health outcomes include emotional distress immediately after abortion, sadness, loneliness, shame, guilt, grief, doubt, and regret. Women who had abortions experienced mental health disorders 30% more often compared to women who had not had an abortion. There was a 25% elevated risk of anxiety, and studies pointed to 10% of the prevalence of mental health

[14]   Pike, G (2017) Abortion and Women's Health https://www.spuc.org.uk/publications-library/750-abortion-and-womens-health-april-2017-pdf/file accessed 13 August 2019

disorders coming from induced abortion. Some women developed PTSD following abortion.

Dr Pike helpfully identifies the difficulties in drawing conclusions from these studies by quoting from one researcher who stated that:

"[There is a] … truly shameful and systematic bias that permeates the psychology of abortion. Professional organisations in the USA and elsewhere have arrogantly sought to distort the scientific literature and paternalistically deny women the information they deserve to make fully informed healthcare choices and receive necessary mental health counselling when and if an abortion decision proves detrimental."[15]

In her book, *"Giving Sorrow Words: the unspoken pain of abortion"* Melinda Tankard – Reist describes the abortion experience of 18 women. She concludes that "It is not enough to tell a woman she might "feel sad for a few days" and that such feelings are "hormonal and will pass," which was the reductionist message on abortion after-effects given to most of this book's contributors. She needs to know she might experience what the women in this book experienced—a long-lasting mental and emotional backlash, and, in some cases, significant physical ramifications—even if the clinic staff don't think these possibilities worth mentioning."[16]

A further aspect of the psychological impact of abortion that is rarely mentioned is the effect of abortion on the father of the child. This is described by Megan Best in her book, *"Fearfully and wonderfully made"*.[17] In her chapter on Abortion she includes a section entitled, "Fathers Hurt Too" in which she describes the grief of novelist Peter Carey

---

[15]   Coleman PK (2012) Author reply to "Abortion and mental health: guidelines for proper scientific conduct ignored." The British Journal of Psychiatry 200:74-83.

[16]   Tankard Reist, M. Giving Sorrow Words, Duffy and Snellgrove, Potts Point, 2000

[17]   Best, M. Fearfully and Wonderfully Made, Matthian Media, Kingsford, NSW, 2012. pp:176-177

"over babies lost through abortion and subsequent miscarriages (due to damage to his first wife's cervix during the abortion procedures)."

In its Position Statement on Women's Health in Relation to Induced Abortion 14 March, 2008, the Royal College of Psychiatrists, London stated that, "The specific issue of whether or not induced abortion has harmful effects on women's mental health remains to be fully resolved. The current research evidence base is inconclusive – some studies indicate no evidence of harm, whilst other studies identify a range of mental disorders following abortion."[18]

However, the statement then recommends that, "Healthcare professionals who assess or refer women who are requesting an abortion should assess for mental disorder and for risk factors that may be associated with its subsequent development. If mental disorder or risk factors are identified, there should be a clearly identified care pathway whereby the mental health needs of the woman and her significant others may be met. The Royal College of Psychiatrists recognises that good practice in relation to abortion will include informed consent. Consent cannot be informed without the provision of adequate and appropriate information regarding the possible risks and benefits to physical and mental health."[19]

While scientific studies can be found to support both the positive and negative links of abortion to psychological distress, one cannot ignore the evidence that pregnancy and its termination impact the emotions of the mother and in many cases these effects are long-lasting.

In the stories to come, Sandy uses the term, "post-abortion syndrome" in her story. This condition is a variant of post-traumatic

---

[18]   Abortion and Mental Health: Cambridge Core. https://www.cambridge.org/core/journals/psychiatric-bulletin/article/abortion-and-mental-health/33C-1F97815738ADFD60A1EA04D5CB725/core-reader accessed 14 August 2019.
[19]   Ibid.

stress disorder (PTSD) used by American psychologist, Vincent Rue to describe PTSD symptoms which he has observed in post-abortive women.[20]

In another story, Madeleine states that, "I was flooded with relief, but also with another unexpected emotion that would reveal itself in time. The discharge pamphlet I read as we drove home promised I would feel a little sad for the next few days because of the hormones, but nothing more. So, I didn't feel sad. I didn't allow myself; I buried everything." As her story reveals, it was only years later that she was able to make sense of the anxiety and depression she experienced following the abortion. Amidst the multitude of scientific studies performed one needs to ask, "How is it possible to measure adequately the complexity and time frame of our human emotions and responses?"

In conclusion, it has been demonstrated that pre-abortion counselling needs to address the reality of the possible risk of mental health issues as a consequence of abortion and include this information when advising women. Medical practitioners must be prepared to acknowledge and warn of these possible risks and make appropriate referral for counselling when mental health issues are identified. As Melinda Tankard Reist correctly identifies, "Informed consent means that, prior to the decision to have an abortion, the patient must be fully advised of all physical and psychological risks associated with abortion, even if the doctor considers those risks minimal."[21] Leaving the final word to Dr. Pike, "Women considering an abortion must be provided with accurate information about the procedure and its possible effects on their health – not least because

---

[20]   Speckhard, Anne, PhD; Rue, Vincent, PhD.Pre- and Peri-natal Psychology Journal; New York Vol. 8, Iss. 1, (Fall 1993).

[21]   Tankard Reist, M. Giving Sorrow Words, Duffy and Snellgrove, Potts Point, 2000

it is most often carried out on healthy women".[22]

For women finding themselves experiencing any of the psychological symptoms mentioned in this chapter there is help available from organisations who provide post abortion grief counselling and support. Some of these organisations are listed at the end of this book on the Resources page.

---

[22]   Pike, G (2017) Abortion and Women's Health https://www.spuc.org.uk/publications-library/750-abortion-and-womens-health-april-2017-pdf/file accessed 13 August 2019

Emma's Story

It's been about 27 years since my first abortion. I was a naive 16-year-old who got ushered off to an abortion clinic by my boyfriend and his father, now having virtually no memory at all as to the details of what happened. Pain, grief and trauma will do that to a person.

What I can tell you is that, when my eyes opened in that "recovery" room, I was forever a different person – because not only a baby was killed inside of me that day, but part of my soul died as well. But nobody else could see that part of me died too because I became very good at hiding my pain.

Repeat Abortions

Something else grew, and that was an unhealthy, obsessive desire to get pregnant again to replace my baby. You would think that after suffering so much grief the last thing you would want to do would be to get pregnant again, particularly when your circumstances were exactly the same.

But get pregnant I did, again and again. Unfortunately, this is an all-too-familiar cycle for many post-abortive women. I found myself often playing out the same scenario of an "unplanned" pregnancy to a man who didn't want a bar of being a father. All I wanted to do was replace my babies. But time and time again I found myself back at an abortion clinic.

Lack of Holistic Counselling

The truth is, in the absolute deepest part of my soul, the last thing I wanted to do was to have another abortion. So why couldn't I get out of the cycle? And why didn't anyone, particularly at an abortion clinic, ask me what was going on? They just booked me in, took my money, gave me a quick five minute "counselling" session and the rest was history.

Psychological Harm

As the years went on, in order to suppress the worsening pain, I went on antidepressants and started seeing psychiatrists, psychologists and counsellors. And not one person asked if I'd had an abortion. Did they not know the damage it does to women? Does anyone know? I found myself having gone from a super-fit, happy and healthy teenager, to an excessive alcohol and drug user, leading a promiscuous lifestyle, still desperately trying to fill the void of that lost child. But no drink, pill or man could ever replace my babies. And nothing could ever turn back the years and turn me into that same girl.

I was lost, desperately miserable, struggling with suicidal tendencies and a self-loathing that was beyond words. I was self-destructing and on a downward spiral, and I knew it. But I didn't know what to do, so I kept numbing myself with alcohol and drugs until one day I could do it no more.

Healing

I started to really look inward and see where the pain was coming from. The healing journey has been slow – very, very slow. One of the countless problems with abortion is that it is almost impossible to find out the truth about the extent to which it harms women. Because, as research by Dr Theresa Burke in her book *Forbidden Grief* shows, during the post-abortion journey, many women will completely deny ever having had an abortion, and then completely deny that it has affected them in any negative way. I can tell you that abortion greatly and deeply affects many women.

Support is Imperative

As a community, let's stand together and support women with unplanned pregnancies. Let's show each woman that having a baby is something that she can do, that she won't be alone but will be supported. The last thing she wants to hear is "I'll support you in whatever you want to do", or "You can't have this baby." Who do we think we are to tell her that? It's a natural instinctive reaction, on a very deep level, for a woman to want to have her baby. It's up to us to help her through the process, regardless of the situation. I only wish, in all of the unplanned pregnancies I faced, that just one person had said that to me. No one ever did. They coerced, forced or abused me into having an abortion, and then left me alone to carry the grief and trauma myself.

Christine's Story

For 34 years I have lived and will continue to live with the regret, heartache and shame of having an abortion. I rationalised my decision by the following: my pregnancy wasn't planned, I was in a new relationship, I wasn't in a financial position to raise a child on my own and if I did it would have brought shame on my family.

I was 25, in a new relationship, taking the pill and I thought I was being responsible. Therefore it came as a total shock that I was pregnant. Adoption wasn't a possibility; I was living away from home and locked in a 12 month lease. The only way to hide my pregnancy was by having an abortion. Back then I was told it was just cells, it wasn't a life and I believed the medical professionals.

The first person I confided in was my flat mate and then an older work colleague who gave me the name of a private gynaecologist and kindly took me to the appointment. I told my boyfriend that this was my body, my choice, my decision. I pretty much shut him out. I had never felt so scared and conflicted. I explained my situation to the doctor and was soon booked in for a Friday afternoon abortion. This allowed me the weekend to recover with no need to take time off work and no one would find out. Sadly my decision came down to what was convenient for me. Lack of finances and how others would perceive me overruled the guilt I felt but it would soon be over and I could put it all behind me. How wrong would that be!

Life Threatening Complications

Hours after being discharged from the hospital I had complications. I was writhing in pain and had a raging temperature and bleeding. My flat mate was distraught. She rang the private hospital but they told her to ring the doctor. He told her to ring a locum or take me to the nearest public hospital. I begged her not to. I was afraid that what I had done would be exposed, so she called a locum who immediately rang for an ambulance. My situation was serious. I was admitted into the intensive care unit (ICU) with septicaemia. My parents had to be notified as it was life threatening. The ambulance ride and how long I was in ICU is still a blur but not the vivid memory of waking to see the worry and concern on my parents' faces. I desperately pleaded with the doctors and nurses not to tell my parents. This was undeniably the most stressful time I had ever experienced. Thankfully the diagnosis of septicaemia, blood poisoning caused through a bacterial infection, satisfied my concerned parents. No other details were given to them.

Not Just Cells

If I thought the worst was over I was sadly mistaken. Physically I would recover but mentally I would not. The enormity of what I had done was about to be realised. Not long after I had been moved into a ward the abdominal pains and bleeding started again. I was assured this was normal as they had given me something to remove any retained products. The nurse left me with a bed pan and to call if I passed anything. It wasn't long before I started passing large blood clots which were taken away for examination. I was so confused as to what was happening to me. How did I get blood poisoning? No one would tell me. They just kept saying that they had contacted my doctor and that he should be in to see me but he never came. It was a nurse who informed me that I had passed an arm and legs. I didn't hear much after that. I felt sick, horrified and in shock. How was that possible? I was told it was just cells! How could I possibly have passed what she said? What had I done?

Regret

My secret sin escalated into a cover up of endless lies to friends, family and work colleagues as I needed to spend several days in hospital and take time off work to recover. Over the years whenever thoughts of what I had done would arise I managed to suppress them but I could never suppress what the nurse had disclosed to me. That image has haunted me to this day and forever will. Unfortunately now, when I do want to remember certain things, in order to put things right, I can't. If you were to ask me the date I found out I was pregnant or even the month, I could not tell you. I believe I did this in order not to have to relive my biggest regret. This was my survival mode. I will live with this for the rest of my life because I was told it was my body and my choice but who was speaking up for the life inside me? With the technology we now have we know babies feel pain inside the womb.

Since this time I have become a Christian and know that God graciously forgives me. However, I struggled to forgive myself until I went to a healing retreat. It was run by beautiful, compassionate, understanding women who gently took me from a place of guilt, shame, resentment, anger, brokenness and unforgiveness to a place of complete healing. This is my story and I want to share this with women who have experienced abortion in the hope that they too will find healing.

Madeleine's Story

I don't remember much about the day I had my abortion. What does remain are crystal clear fragments of memories and a little stone I keep as a memento in a locked box and take out sometimes to remind myself of that day. Trauma is complicated and so much of that day has been buried beneath my coping mechanisms.

I remember driving up to that cheerful yellow clinic and once inside trying to make small talk while I waited for my appointment. The girl beside me, only a little older than me, casually admitted that this was her sixth abortion. She didn't seem to have any qualms about this. I'd never even considered that people could end up here twice. I was confused, wasn't this the last resort? She seemed nonchalant about the whole thing, but I found myself internally vowing to never end up here again.

False Information

I do remember sitting with the so-called counsellor. She seemed kind and genuinely concerned when she asked me if I had any worries. "I guess I'm just worried about the baby's stage of development," I said. She smiled, "There's no need to be worried: it's not a baby!" She assured me confidently. "It's only a ball of cells no bigger than half the size of your little fingernail." As she held her hand up to illustrate, I breathed a sigh of relief and tried to quiet my churning stomach with this 'fact'.

After it was all over, I woke up groggy from the general anaesthetic that I'd asked my mother to pay for so I wouldn't remember what happened. I was covered in a hand crocheted blanket, its bright colours a stark contrast to the white walls and sterility around me. Then I suddenly realised that for the first time in months I no longer felt nauseous; I finally felt like myself again. I was flooded with relief, but also with another unexpected emotion that would reveal itself in time. The discharge pamphlet I read as we drove home promised I would feel a little sad for the next few days because of the hormones, but nothing more. So, I didn't feel sad. I didn't allow myself; I buried everything.

These fragments are all that remains other than the blood red stone I picked up in the car park as I walked out, a commemoration chosen unwittingly to symbolise that bloody day. I keep it still. Running my hands over its cold, smooth surface reminds me of that day, all those years ago in a cold stark room, when I found myself alone again, relieved but profoundly empty. There was no life left inside my womb.

Grief

Over the sixteen years since I terminated my first child's life, I have grown more and more aware of that unplanned, unexpected, unidentified grief. I have named it for what it is, just as I have named my baby, Azaliah. She is the person who is missing in every family photo, on every adventure, the shadow of a past I'll never outrun. I don't want to.

Misinformed

I found myself unexpectedly pregnant at 18. I had to make my decision alone, yet I was surrounded by supporters. The irony of my situation is that it was a case of blind privilege. I was well educated and intelligent having just completed Year 12 at a wonderful, supportive private girls' school. Neither my boyfriend nor either set of parents pressured me to have the abortion. Instead, from the people I loved and trusted there was eerie silence. They said nothing except that they'd support me whatever my choice. Yet I expected opposition. I acted confidently about my choice but I was anything but sure. I was young, naive and misinformed but I'm not any more.

It took me so long to understand what happened that day because the whole experience was shrouded in half-truths. It was as I sat in an anatomy and physiology lesson in first year nursing, staring blankly at the embryonic development of a ten-week-old foetus, that the whole house of lies came crashing down around me. There she was: no ball of cells, no half a fingernail-sized blob but a baby, heartbeat and all. I could hear my heart beating in my head, an echo of the thousands of tears I'd shed since that day four years earlier but never realised were for her. I didn't understand how they could have been. I had genuinely believed there was no baby, just a ball of cells. My head tried to convince my heart but it didn't believe. My body knew it carried so much more than a blob. The anxiety and depression developed after I stopped the baby's development.

I was pregnant with pain, but it took years for it to give birth to grief and meanwhile it swelled unhealthily inside. I was bloated with it, unnaturally distended with pain. That moment of realisation broke me open, and I found within a well of grief so immense. There was no escape from the horror of accepting what I had done to my firstborn child. I was terrified that facing it would mean falling into a chasm of tears from which I feared I could never emerge.

But I have emerged. Forgiveness and healing have transformed my grief into a confident belief that what happened to me was terribly wrong and that what I did was kill my child. I signed away her life with less awareness than when I signed the countless pages of warnings for a recent routine endoscopy.

In the name of wanting to be supportive of a young woman facing an unexpected pregnancy, a young woman at risk of feeling pressured and condemned; the risks were never even mentioned. Not by the doctor I visited, not by the counsellor and not by the abortionist. It was decided for me by society that I didn't need the difficult facts, because abortion was the best choice for all involved. On the form the counsellor filled out she wrote that I had decided that "abortion is the best option for Madeleine and her baby." The irony; it should have said for Madeleine and her "ball of cells".

Regret

Since coming to understand what happened that day, I have been struck by the stories that were all around me as I made my choice. So many of the people who I believed supported my decision actually cared deeply about the unborn and didn't believe abortion was the best choice but felt they couldn't or shouldn't speak. My parents would have done anything to save the life of their first child, whom they lost because of a medical mistake during my mother's labour. They still grieve for her today and they could have informed my decision if they'd felt free to speak.

My boyfriend's mother could have spoken life to me, too. She had kept her baby, the father of my unborn child, despite being pressured to abort. He was the product of a violent and abusive relationship, but she said keeping him was the best decision she ever made, and she was so sorry that she didn't tell me his story then. I wish I had shared about my pregnancy with my half-sister, Sarah. She was the product of my Dad's university fling but she was adopted. When we became friends later in life, it showed that adoption could be a doorway to future life and joy. Sarah later told me she would have done anything to help me keep the baby, even adopting it herself. Her tears of regret when I told her caused a new wave of tears for me, as I realised how different this all could have ended if only we had all understood and acknowledged the truth, and been brave enough to speak.

I have many regrets, but the one thing I don't regret is telling my story. I hope that by sharing what happened to me, my story will echo in the ears of others facing the same decision and perhaps help them to make a different one.

As I look at my children today, I realise that life, messy and complicated as it is, would be better with Azaliah. She was an opportunity to laugh, to learn, to grow, to stretch and groan with labour. With her birth, beauty would have been born from my pain, instead of grief being conceived from termination.

Sonya's Story[23]

In society we are told many things and one of them is the lie that abortion is ok. It's presented as a practical option and sold as the complete right of the mother to choose whether her baby lives or dies. The slogan 'my body my choice' is widely known. I wish I never heard it.

Finding myself pregnant at 20 years old was not in my plan. I was very against the idea of abortion and frequently shared my opinions on the matter.

Mine wasn't a tragic childhood filled with abuse, loss or total rejection but I never felt quite like I belonged or was loved or valued. I know, now, that my parents did the best they knew how.

No Counselling or Support

At this time in my life I would have classified myself as a typical teenage girl trying to find love in all the wrong places. Yes, plenty of alcohol and partying filled my days in the hope I would be popular and fit in. I have no excuse for my selfish decision. My heart wanted to keep the baby, my head said no. In short, my boyfriend didn't want a child so my head won and we aborted. From this moment on my life would never be the same.

I didn't talk to anyone about it, not even my boyfriend. I had no counselling or support at any time. So life went on. I struggled internally with many emotions including pain, hurt, disgust at myself

---

[23] Name changed to preserve anonymity

and shame. So, so, so ashamed of what I had done. How could I tell anyone? They would hate me.

Depression

A few years later I found myself suffering from depression. I didn't know why or even recognize that it was depression. I just thought the world hated me, everyone hated me and my new husband hated me. Life was just awful. I pushed on.

After a few years of my marriage I suffered a miscarriage, but was then blessed with two beautiful children. They became my world and I loved them dearly. Unfortunately I was still suffering from depression and eventually my marriage dissolved. I thought it was entirely my husband's fault and found it easy to blame him. I do remember crying out to God in the shower one morning, just before my marriage fell apart and asking God to please take me out of this mess. I was literally crying and sitting on the floor in the shower, confused, unloved, alone, with two little kids to care for, crying out to God to help me. At the time I felt my prayer fell on deaf ears. Life went on, but now I see it was from this point that things did start to change. It took a long while, but I'm so far from whom I was then that I know changes began to happen then.

Second Abortion

My journey continued and I moved on. Now on my own as a single mum, trying desperately to do the right thing but still longing to be loved and cared for. After a few years I found myself pregnant again! I was devastated! I didn't want another child to another man and become a typical single mum with kids from different dads, living in a housing trust home, judged by the world, society and by my family. There was no way I could have that child. Long story short, I aborted again.

I didn't tell anyone, once again. My boyfriend knew, but he didn't want a child either. When I went in for the procedure they took an ultrasound. I didn't look. I remember being disgusted at myself and angry that I wasn't brave enough to do this. I was screaming on the inside and as I waited to be wheeled into the theatre I remember saying over and over again in my head, "I'm sorry God, I'm sorry God, I'm just so sorry, I just don't know what else to do, I can't do this, I'm too weak, I'm just so sorry."

Deeper Depression

Very soon after this abortion I fell into a deep depression. Struggling to keep up with two toddlers on my own, I was self-medicating with alcohol of an evening when the kids went to bed in the hope it would numb me.

With thoughts of abandoning my life I finally fell on my knees and cried out to God again. This time I was serious. I remember the words something like, "God, if you really love me the way people say you do, and if you can really make such a difference in my life, if you can do a better job of it than me then I'm done! I quit. I give up. I give my life to you because I've made such a mess that I don't want to do it anymore. It's up to you now. If you are as good as you say you are then please fix this, take over, I'm done!"

Soon after I started attending church and was baptized. For a while I struggled through more depression, anxiety, self-hatred, condemnation, fear and shame.

Finally I sought some counselling and the miraculous happened. In a counselling session I asked God to please look after the children I had aborted, to love them & accept them into heaven as it wasn't their fault that I had ended their lives.

Suddenly I had a vision…. I was standing on a beautiful grassy hill, grass as soft as you've ever felt, a gentle warm breeze, the sunshine warming my face; it was my kind of place. Looking down the hill as I stood on the side I could see Jesus surrounded with children, a few at the front and many behind. He was walking toward me. He was holding a little boy, about two years old.

Standing next to him was a girl, possibly around twelve years old. I couldn't see the other children, or rather I wasn't looking at them, but I could see Jesus & these two children clearly. They were looking at me with love in their eyes and Jesus said, "It's okay, I've got them. They are safe & happy here with me, they are not lost." That's all that was said.

It was but a glimpse and then the vision was gone, but they were beautiful, so beautiful. These were my children. I can't describe the absolute joy at knowing that they were safe, that they were not lost forever. At this time I also named my children 'Sophie' and 'Joseph'. I have no idea where these names came from but I hope they are appropriate.

So my journey to healing was now in full motion.

I have now been healed from depression completely and although life still throws many challenges at me I now finally have a peace about my lost children.

I find myself at a point in life now where I am wanting God to use me in any way He can to help others (both men and women) who have been affected by abortion and to show them Gods healing grace so they too can live life free from shame and self-condemnation.

Past mistakes and regrets fester into nasty poisonous wounds that become larger than we can handle. I don't want us to buy this abortion lie anymore. It's time to expose this procedure for what it is. It's a crime against women as much as the unborn child.

Sandy's Story[24]

When I am asked to tell my story about my abortion, I must mentally prepare myself because no matter how many times I talk or write about it, it doesn't get any easier.

As I take myself back to my first abortion experience, I am lying on the hospital bed as the surgeon is running the ultrasound on my stomach to determine how many weeks pregnant I am so a method of termination can be determined. I glance at the monitor and I pause, watching my baby's heartbeat. If I could have told my 26-year-old self then what I know now, I would have told her of the shame, guilt, depression, and despair she would have for many years afterward. I would have told her not to make the biggest mistake she will ever make in her life.

I am now 45, married with four children and I have a happy life. I love being a mother and a wife. I have wonderful close relationships with family and friends but only a handful of them know of the deep heartache I carry.

As a teenager in senior school I had a very strong opinion about abortion. I felt that abortion was never an option in any circumstance. I was so passionate about it that as part of my Year 11 English studies I wrote an assignment for a persuasive piece. Abortion was never going to be an option for me.

My first daughter was born by emergency caesarean section at 28 weeks gestation due to pre-eclampsia. She weighed 900 grams. After her birth I was in Intensive Care for 36 hours and I was told she had a fifty percent chance of surviving. If she did survive, she could have many difficulties such as Cerebral Palsy, oxygen dependence and lung disease. She did survive and while she was on oxygen for five weeks and at 10 weeks needed a blood transfusion due to anaemia, she had no other medical problems at all. However, it was a very stressful and scary time as she was my first baby and the whole experience was traumatic.

Aborting with Post Natal Depression

Twelve months after my daughter was born, I fell pregnant and I instantly went into a panic. I was terrified of getting pre-eclampsia again, as the doctors said that was likely. The thought of going through that traumatic experience again was all I could think about. I was still recovering from the birth of my daughter. I felt I had failed her because she was in hospital for three months so I couldn't breast feed her or bond with her. Looking back I realize I had post-natal depression. This led me to feel that I had no option but to have an abortion. Because I was so terribly ill with morning sickness and trying to look after a 12-month-old and my 6-year-old step-daughter, I felt it was my only option.

I recall telling the counsellor at the abortion clinic my reasons and all she recommended was if after the termination I feel like I had made the wrong choice, to see my doctor for anti-depressants. Reflecting, as a counsellor, she should have recognized my symptoms of post-natal depression.

My husband came to pick me up from the abortion clinic with my daughter and a bunch of flowers. I felt an emptiness but was relieved that my nausea was gone and I could now get on with my life. I kept pushing that feeling of emptiness down. This led me to self-medicate with marijuana which helped with the pain. It took away the low feeling and helped me to get on with my day but unfortunately I became very addicted. Smoking marijuana also lead me to mindlessness and I became very apathetic.

Second Abortion

I fell pregnant again and because I didn't want to stop smoking marijuana or drinking heavily during the day, I went through with my second abortion.

Third and Fourth Abortion

Over the next three years I had two more abortions at different locations because I didn't want the staff seeing me have more than one abortion. After my last abortion I hit a low. Nothing worked anymore to ease the mental pain and I was very unhappy. My marriage was falling apart, and our life was spiralling out of control.

Through our daughters being enrolled in a Christian school, my husband and I took part in a course which explained what our daughters would be learning regarding religion. Through this course, my husband and I took the gift of God's love into our life and started to live a 'cleaner' lifestyle. Towards the end of the course I fell pregnant again and while termination was my first thought and although I initially felt fear and was worried about pre-eclampsia, I knew I wanted to have this baby. My son was born at 34 weeks by emergency caesarean due to pre-eclampsia. Eighteen months later I had a baby girl, born at full-term. Our lives had changed for the better, we were no longer living like sad, broken people and the life we used to live seemed hard to believe.

Six years ago, I watched a movie titled 'October Baby' which is a true story about a girl who had survived an abortion and was adopted.

As I began to watch this movie, I had no idea of the impact it would have on me. It reminded me of my past and my abortions which I had not thought about for years. I thought they hadn't had any impact on me, that it was in my past and I was a better person now.

I cried for a couple of hours. My husband cried with me and we talked about the abortions for the first time.

Although this was difficult, I thought I was able to put it all in perspective and move on but about a year after watching that movie I had my first anxiety attack. I was in the baby aisle in the supermarket looking for a gift for a friend who had just had a baby. Going down the baby aisle is something I've always loved; the smell of the baby powder and the cute baby toys always reminded me of when my children were babies. This time though I found myself unable to think straight, my chest was tight, I felt my face and neck burning up and I had to get out of there.

I had to avoid the baby aisle from that day. If I walked past the aisle I couldn't look down it. I was living with a deep sense of shame, sadness, anxiety and depression. I experienced daily feelings of loss and I could not bring myself to think about the precious lives I had chosen to end before they had a chance to enter this world. I found myself unable to hold a newborn baby or share in the joy of a friend's birth announcement without feeling overwhelming anxiety. I was angry and I had no self-worth.

Post Abortion Syndrome

My anxiety grew worse and one day after I said some awful things to my husband during an argument, I googled my symptoms. What came up on the screen hit me hard. I had Post Abortion Syndrome. I continued to research and I was amazed at how familiar the stories were of other women going through the same experience. I came across a support group which offered support and counselling for women suffering from Post Abortion Syndrome. There was information about a retreat which was tailored for the purpose of healing women, affected by abortion but the retreat was not offered in Adelaide.

For a year or so I continued to struggle on with my pain and anxiety. One night I went out with a group of women, one of whom had just had a baby. When I walked in, she handed the baby to me, presuming I wanted to have a cuddle with the precious new life. I became completely overcome with fear and didn't know how to react. If I decline holding the baby what excuse do I give? If I show how I'm feeling people will need an explanation. I couldn't even look down at this little baby boy in my arms.

I walked into another room away from people so no-one would notice the tears in my eyes. I pulled myself together, walked back and handed the baby to someone else as I hurried off to the toilet. I sat in the toilet for about ten minutes crying, trying to breathe through my anxiety. After this night I decided I had to do something. I thought about how there would be other times when I would come across newborn babies, even my own grandchildren one day and then what was I going to do?

I went to see a couple who were close friends, told them everything, and through them I learnt that the support group had just started a retreat in Adelaide, so they booked me in.

I attended the retreat two years ago and although I knew it would be helpful in my healing process, I had no idea the importance of allowing myself to grieve the babies I had lost, naming them and saying goodbye. I cannot explain how valuable the retreat has been and how the shame was lifted from my heart. The counsellors helped me to face and process my emotions. They helped me release myself of the guilt and hurt I had been holding on to and showed me so much love without judgement. Although I am doing better and the anxiety is not as debilitating, I do still suffer in silence. I miss my children whom I never had a chance to meet and I live with the fact I chose to end the lives of four human beings. Whenever I hear the word abortion my heart skips a beat and my chest tightens.

No woman should go through what I have been through; it is unnecessary and traumatic. I appreciate that pregnancies are not always wanted. I know pregnancy is sometimes the result of painful situations. Pregnancy can be inconvenient and life changing and if you aren't prepared for it, it can be very daunting. However, if women who decide to abort their child knew of the despair and anguish to follow, they would agree abortion isn't the solution they believed would simply remove the evidence of a pregnancy. Unfortunately, the memory stays with you forever.

Rose's Story[25]

When I was just 21 years old I found myself pregnant. I didn't know the father of the baby very well and didn't believe there would be a future with him. I didn't know what to do so I told my mother. She told me outright that the shame of it would kill my father. That wasn't what I needed to hear. I felt so alone and didn't know who else to reach out to.

What were the options? There were not many available to me. I wanted to keep my baby but to do so I would need to move interstate and either put my baby up for adoption or keep my baby knowing that I would not see my family again. I was beside myself. It was such a huge inner struggle. I was so full of turmoil not knowing what to do.

"Easy Option"

I went to see my doctor to confirm the pregnancy which he did. Then to my surprise without a moment's hesitation he gave me the option of an abortion at 12 weeks. I remember being quite surprised that he would suggest that. It seemed all too easy, all my problems solved, no one needed to know and I was free to continue my life as normal. I couldn't believe I was given such an easy option. I had been in turmoil and abortion being legal made the problem with my pregnancy go away. I grappled with what to do but all of a sudden I was given this easy option.

I couldn't keep my baby which was what I really wanted because everything seemed stacked against me. What made matters worse was that while I was waiting for the abortion I was getting so very much attached to this little presence that I felt growing inside me. Yet there was no one on my side, no one I could turn to in order to share those special moments with or who would even care. It was heartbreaking. As I came closer to having the abortion I found the bonding between us increase and it became very hard. I was in a real state of panic.

Dissociation

In order to be able to go through with the abortion I actually had to make a decision and that was to convince myself, to harden myself and divorce myself from what I was feeling. I had to make myself become cold blooded toward the baby I was carrying. I knew there was no other way I could do this. I told myself that abortion was legal therefore it couldn't be as bad as I thought. I made myself believe what the law saw my foetus as, just a clump of cells. If they believed that, then I made myself believe that. It was an absolutely terrible time. I would not allow myself to connect with my baby and it was so hard because every part of me wanted to feel the opposite deep down inside. I so wanted to keep my baby.

Even now as I write this the memories of that struggle come back so vividly to me. Words can't express how choosing to reject my child's life still haunts me. I remember just wanting the abortion to happen because I was finding it so hard to live the lie. I felt guilt that my baby was paying the price so that my life could go back to normal. It seemed so unfair and l felt so selfish.

The day I went to the abortion clinic I sat in the lobby with my mother. I just waited till my name was called. At the actual abortion, as I was lying there, I had to convince myself that this was just a normal procedure like having your tonsils removed. I made light conversation with the nurse. I then had to face the horrible truth of the decision I had made.

On the way home we stopped the car because I was dry retching. I stayed in bed for two days recuperating and most of that time was spent staring into space. I had never experienced such profound emptiness, sorrow and regret.

I had to face the fact that l had done something to a part of me and my inner being that was irreparable. I had nowhere to hide from myself. I still live like that. You learn eventually to bury who you really know yourself to be but it never truly goes away. The memory is there for a lifetime; engraved into your innermost being. You can't escape it.

After that a profound change happened within me. I knew something significant in me had died along with my child. Deep negative emotions about myself started to rise up; these replaced the positive outlook I had on life. My mother and I never spoke about it. I never spoke to anyone about it. It remained buried as my soul's silent secret.

My future outlook changed after that day. I self-sabotaged any positive prospects that may have presented themselves in my life. I didn't believe I deserved anything good to happen to me. I still struggle with that even now.

Depression

When I was 25 I became seriously depressed. I didn't understand what was happening to me. I felt I had no control over my life and that there was no future. It lasted for over two years. I was on medication during that time. Only later did I find out that depression is often linked with abortion.

Much later on I married, but the shame of what I had done stopped me from sharing it with my husband. I didn't think he would understand so it stayed buried.

I found it difficult to bond with my firstborn child and I didn't know why. My second born child was preterm at 34 weeks and lived for only 20 hours due to complications at birth. At this time the memories flooded in and the torment began. I still didn't have the conversation with my husband that I should have had. It was harder now because I now blamed myself for my son's death. I saw it as divine retribution. I took a life and a life had been taken from me and the deep sense of shame was now too great. Our marriage didn't last. I was consumed with tremendous grief and guilt and felt I was spiralling out of control. No one could help me. I never remarried because I didn't believe I could trust anyone with my secret who would understand.

In 2014 I heard a man talking about how his mother tried to abort him. That was the first time in 40 years that I had heard anyone speak about what I considered to be a taboo subject. It gave me the confidence to tell some close friends. It took me two years after that to build up the courage to tell my own children.

The abortion had ended my pregnancy at 12 weeks. My life seemingly went back to being normal, but on deeper levels my life was very much impacted by that decision to terminate my pregnancy. That decision had such a negative impact on my life. It caused a lot of pain to many people who didn't deserve it. The decision I made continues to haunt me to this day. I often look back and think what appeared to be the easy option was actually a smoking mirror.

Life

The following four stories illustrate situations in which women chose to continue their pregnancies despite being offered, and in one case seriously considering, abortion. Their reasons for refusing abortion are varied which demonstrates the complexity of women's lives and indeed the complexity of the issue of abortion.

In his review, *Abortion and Women's Health*, Dr. Greg Pike included studies which demonstrated that some women chose motherhood despite, "difficulties they faced and despite the negative assumptions of health professionals".[26] In the following stories, despite the obvious difficulties that each of the pregnancies presented to the women involved, seeing their pregnancy through to birth and ultimately motherhood, brought hope and joy.

This is not to negate the obvious challenges that an unplanned pregnancy affords. In the case of unplanned pregnancy, Dr Pike identifies in his review the essential role of social service agencies and their "ongoing role to foster and support development for mothers and their children and to assist with avoidance of repetitive cycles of family trauma."[27] Mothers need to be supported by these social service agencies or non-government agencies to provide material assistance as well as emotional support.

Some agencies which are available to help women who find themselves in the sitiuation of an unplanned pregnancy are listed in the Resources page at the end of this book.

---

[26]   Pike, G (2017) Abortion and Women's Health https://www.spuc.org.uk/publications-library/750-abortion-and-womens-health-april-2017-pdf/file accessed 13 August 2019

[27]   Ibid

Stacey's Story

When I found out I was pregnant at 16, it wasn't exactly how I expected my final year of high school to pan out.

I'd only been with my boyfriend for four months. The condom broke one night, Valentine's Day actually. But no problem. We went to the emergency room of our local hospital and I took the morning after pill. Phew, I thought, I'm so glad there are options like this available.

But then a few weeks passed, and I had a suspicion that I might be pregnant, I just felt different. Not wanting to entertain the thought or believe my worst fear I pushed it to the back of my mind and carried on as normal. But I couldn't let it go. I did a pregnancy test, which came up negative. What a relief! Little did I know that condoms, morning after pills and pregnancy tests aren't 100% accurate. Sure, they might make those disclaimers but surely it wouldn't happen to me, or so I thought.

Weeks later I couldn't deny it any longer. At 18 weeks pregnant I began to feel my daughter moving inside of me.

Shock, fear, panic and shame gripped me. This couldn't be happening! I was always a good girl; at least down in the depths of my heart I knew what was right. I'd been raised in a Christian home. I went to church with my parents. I was only having a bit of fun, nothing unlike what all my friends and peers around me were doing. My worst fears were confirmed with a second pregnancy test. What now?!

Given No Choice

Overwhelming embarrassment, fear and shame enveloped me. Oh, the shame. I wanted as few people as possible to know about this. The few people I did tell that I was pregnant encouraged me that abortion was the best option; my boyfriend, his parents, my closest girlfriend and the school nurse.

When each of them asked me what I wanted to do, or whether I wanted to keep the baby, I said that I wanted an abortion. I wanted this problem to be fixed and fast. After I'd made my plans known, there was not another word of pursuing an alternative.

The internet and this thing called Google was relatively new at the time, so I googled unplanned pregnancy trying to find out some more information and links for abortion clinics. From my memory, the resources I found all pointed towards abortion. I found a few clinics online, made some enquiries and booked into the one that could fit me in soonest.

There was no suggestion of needing to see my doctor, or having an appointment with a counsellor. This clinic allowed me, a 16 year old girl, to book myself in for an abortion without the need for support or consent from my parents, or anyone else.

Dissociation

When I booked in for the abortion, I could already feel her moving inside of me. How I disconnected myself from this fact, I still don't know; the shock, the fear, the panic, and the shame I guess.

Then I had to tell my parents. That was the worst. But with matters already settled in my mind and heart I told them I was going to have an abortion and was already booked in for a few days' time. I could see their shock and their hearts breaking. They are strongly against abortion and made their position known to me. But, they said that they loved me, and would support me, whatever my decision and the outcome.

Walking into the abortion clinic was one of the worst moments of my life. I felt so overwhelmed. I just wanted to be invisible. I wanted this all to be over, quickly.

I sat in the waiting room and the contrast of how it was decorated and how I was feeling struck me. The waiting room was a bright yellow with so many happy paintings hanging up and fresh flowers scattered around. I wanted to scream. This isn't a happy place, I wanted to yell. I looked around at the other women in the waiting room wondering how they were feeling inside. They all looked so calm and normal, like they were about to go in for some sort of routine check-up. Those moments of waiting and wondering were horrible. Then it was my turn.

As I sat with the doctor for the pre-screening she asked me some brief questions and did an initial scan. She turned to me and said, "Ok, everything looks fine, are you ready?"

Everything looks fine? Everything looks fine? What does that mean? At that moment I asked her if everything with the baby was healthy and ok. She said, "Yes." I asked the doctor if she could tell if it was a boy or a girl. She said, "Yes."

Last Minute Change of Mind

Something inside me, in that moment, changed. What was I doing? I told her I wanted to see the scan. She turned the screen to me and there she was, Katie, 19 weeks, perfect and healthy, sucking her thumb. And I was about to terminate her. I drew on every bit of courage I had which in that moment didn't feel like much, and told her that I didn't want to go through with it. To say things were easy from that moment onwards would be telling a lie, but the huge wave of peace in the depths of my being far outweighed the challenges.

Life is Sweet

Despite my pregnancy, I completed year 12, and went on to complete not just one, but two University degrees in education. I also have numerous other vocational qualifications in health and fitness, and now I run my own holistic health and wellness business. I'm also happily married and the three of us feel like the perfect fit. Truly life is so very sweet. I love my life. And I wouldn't change a thing.

When I found myself in a crisis pregnancy, it may have seemed like my life was over. But I now know that my life, and the life of another, had only really just begun. As I said before, I can't imagine my life without Katie - and when I do, when I think back to how close I was to not having her, it brings me to tears.

This all comes down to the value of life. And I now believe that a life is a life of value with a purpose from the moment of conception. All the goodness that makes Katie was put inside her from the moment she was conceived. No matter how she was conceived, from that moment of conception, she was a life with a purpose, with a personality, and with so many gifts and talents and abilities. I am so grateful the world doesn't miss out on the beauty and flavour of what my Katie girl adds to it.

But what if I had gone along with the suggestion of those strong influences in my world at the time? What if I'd partnered with the stereotype of a teenage pregnancy that society offers? The only portrayal of the situation I found myself in is overwhelmingly negative. The opinions and expectations of someone in my position are certainly anything but positive.

Coercion

I was young and terrified and under great pressure from my partner and his family to go through with the termination. To gain counselling and support and to even be told that there were alternatives and that I was capable to navigate them and even thrive would have been helpful. Abortion should not be offered as my only option.

I am so very grateful my story has a happy ending. But how many other young women find themselves in a crisis pregnancy and like I did, don't have anyone offering them a positive narrative of what their life could look like if they continue with their pregnancy? How many others succumb to the pressure and lack of hope offered in such a situation? How many Katie's does the world miss out on?

Jordanne's Story

On 4th April, 2014, my first obstetric ultrasound was at 22 weeks, delayed due to severe hyperemesis gravidarum, morning sickness. My husband and I were anxious to hear our baby's heart beat for the first time. It was a surreal and long-awaited moment after almost 18 emotional months of trying to fall pregnant and being told of only a 5% chance of conception naturally.

Foetal Abnormality Diagnosis

A moment that was meant to be joyous suddenly turned to heartbreak and despair. Our baby boy was diagnosed with Dandy Walker Malformation with moderate bilateral lateral ventriculomegaly: a brain condition characterised by a small cerebellum, enlargement of the posterior fossa and dilation of the lateral ventricles resulting in excess fluid in the brain.

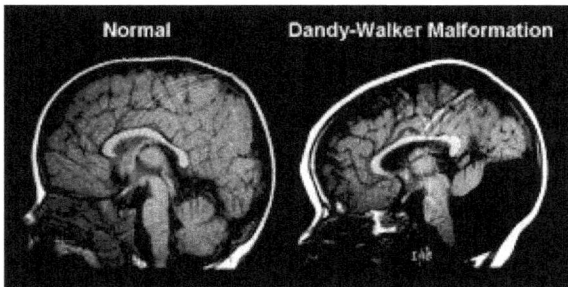

We were told that my son would experience the following:
- Surgery at birth, insertion of a VP Shunt for the drainage of the excess fluid in the brain.

- Developmental delays in motor and language skills such as sitting up, walking, and talking.
- Poor muscle tone, balance, and coordination.
- Problems with eye movement, mainly jerky eye movement.
- Vision and hearing impairment.
- Seizures.

Advised to Abort

With this prognosis we were advised to abort and, given I was already 22 weeks pregnant, we were advised, and even pressured by some medical professionals, to make a quick decision to do so, as the cut off for legal abortion in South Australia is 24 weeks.[28]

Decision to Keep the Baby

Hearing our son's heartbeat for the first time was confirmation to us that we were going to keep our baby, to love and care for him no matter what the diagnosis.

In making this decision, I was regularly monitored with fortnightly ultrasounds up until a few days before my son was born. We were put under the care of the Maternal Foetal Medicine Unit and the Neurology team. Each ultrasound, nine in total, confirmed the diagnosis. At 38 weeks, my son Patrick was born via emergency Caesarean section due to foetal distress.

Healthy Boy

At only a few days old Patrick showed positive signs and passed all Paediatric and Neurological checks. A cranial ultrasound and MRI

---

[28]   Editors' note: The law in South Australia since 1969 is that the general limit for legal abortion is 28 weeks. After that time abortions may only be carried out if the mother's life is in danger.

of the brain and spinal cord were organised. Remarkably, the cranial ultrasound showed "the ventricles are not dilated" and the MRI revealed "no evidence of posterior fossa cystic malformation... thereby excluding the possibility of a Dandy Walker Malformation". There was, however, "evidence of a shortened corpus callosum along with hypoplastic posterior white matter", which is an abnormality or the absence of nerve fibres in the brain.

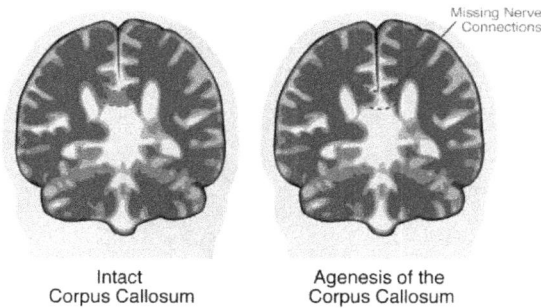

Missing Nerve Connections

Intact
Corpus Callosum

Agenesis of the
Corpus Callosum

This was an outstanding result given the initial diagnosis, despite the evidence of white matter volume loss.

Fast forward five years from his initial diagnosis, Patrick is now a healthy young boy of almost five years. Patrick has been eligible to receive NDIS funding for Speech Therapy, Physiotherapy, Hydrotherapy and Occupational Therapy from six months of age. As a result of these early interventional supports Patrick's Neurologist, at his recent review on November 8th, 2018, "is truly pleased with his neuro-developmental progress and most impressed with his expressive and receptive language which has demonstrated a significant interval development, as has his gross and fine motor abilities."

Patrick's Kindergarten teacher, Michelle, is also pleased with Patrick's progress and development over the last 18 months since commencement at his Early Learning Centre. Michelle's most recent report of Patrick from the May 8th, 2019 affirms this as he topped his Kindergarten class in assessments of language and image recognition. Michelle also states that, "Patrick is highly intelligent."

Even medical professionals cannot be 100% sure of outcomes. Their recommendation, although continuously confirmed through investigations using the best available technology, was to abort my beautiful boy who has since defied all odds.

Miriam's Story

In 2007, my husband, Martin, and I discovered we were expecting our third child. My pregnancy was completely normal. I went to routine doctor appointments for prenatal care just like every other expectant woman. All went well until the 18-week mark. I was receiving my first ultrasound at a hospital. Martin was not able to attend as he was working. This didn't bother me as we wanted to keep the baby's gender a secret anyway. The radiologists hovered over the scans. Minutes ticked by. Having had two children previously, I knew that the radiologists were taking much longer than they usually would. Suddenly a nurse seemed to notice me still lying there.

She told me she was going to talk to a doctor. Confused thoughts whizzed through my mind. Was something wrong with my child? The doctor came back, and having scrutinised the scans in detail, proceeded to speak with a concerned look on his face. There is something abnormal in the child's bowel, he said, we will have to refer you to another hospital to do another ultrasound.

I was then asked to call my husband and was taken to the Women's and Children's Hospital in Adelaide. There, several doctors examined the second ultrasound. The verdict was not good. Scans indicated that the baby could have cystic fibrosis, a serious malfunction of the body's exocrine system that affects the lungs and digestive system. If our child was born with this disease it would have to undergo frequent medical check-ups, treatments and physiotherapy. The doctors were frank. They said that, although they couldn't be certain, the child had about a 75% chance of having cystic fibrosis. For further confirmation, blood tests were taken from both my husband and me.

It showed that I carried a cystic fibrosis gene, while Martin did not. The baby was also abnormally small for an 18-week old. This led doctors to suppose that the abnormality in the baby's bowel could also be another disability, which was possibly stunting her growth. In the meantime, I was asked to come back for weekly scans so the doctors could monitor our child's growth.

Offered Abortion

At 22 weeks, nearing the end of the second trimester, I was sitting in the doctor's office with Martin. The doctor looked us in the eye. "Do you want to abort this child?" Both Martin's and my jaws dropped. Silence reigned as we stared into the doctor's questioning face. He couldn't be serious, or could he? Aborting our child was a thought neither of us had even considered. Unable to speak, we looked at each other.

Finally, we blurted, "No way!" The doctor was taken aback. "Oh, so you don't need to come for the check-ups, as there is nothing we can do for the child anyway."

The pregnancy continued reasonably well, with the exception of the concern about the baby's small size. However, our faith in God carried us through this trial. There were a lot of unknowns but we had decided not to end this precious life and to bear the difficulties that came with having the child.

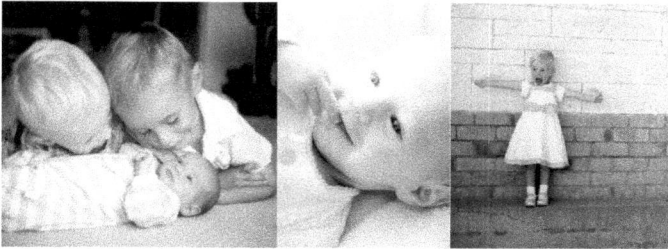

Perfectly Healthy Baby

The last five days of pregnancy were filled with tension. Apart from its still tiny stature, the baby's heart rate was dangerously low. We turned once again to our strong faith in the Giver of all life and prayed for the baby's safety. On 6th February, 2008, a baby girl was born to us. We named her Annelle, which means 'God has favoured me'. Truly He had, because Annelle was not born with cystic fibrosis or any other disability. Instead she is a bright and perfectly healthy child with an irresistible grin.

Lois's Story

(A tribute to two beautiful parents, Laurie and Ailsa)

Mum found she was unexpectedly pregnant with me, and she cried; she was a mother of two small children under two and a half years of age, and she was suffering with severe chronic colitis, an infection of the colon. Her condition was worsening and her GP recommended an abortion. This was in 1958 in country South Australia.

In 1969, legislation was passed to legalise abortion in South Australia 'when necessary to protect the life or physical or mental health of the woman – taking into account the current and reasonably foreseeable future – or in cases when the child was likely to be born with serious handicaps.'

The recommendation to abort me came 11 years before the 1969 legislation. I assume it was a highly unusual recommendation for the time. I don't know if Mum was told she would die if she gave birth to me, but we know the abortion was suggested due to the severity of her health condition.

Mum left the doctors' clinic in horror at the suggestion of abortion. She told me she drove home thinking, "But that would be no different than killing Nita or Joy!" They were my two older toddler sisters, fifteen months apart in age. Mum and Dad believed in the sacredness of human life from the moment of conception.

I was born on Friday 17th July, 1959 at 4.30am in the Naracoorte Hospital, weighing in at 6-pounds 5½- ounces. Dad and Mum named me Lois Margaret.

I am so grateful for Dad and Mum's belief in the sanctity of life for the unborn! I am grateful this was reinforced by the laws of government and societal thinking of that time. I am grateful for the incredibly strong family and community supports that were available to Mum and Dad. I am grateful for their unified, deep faith and trust in Jesus in very difficult circumstances.

I know that many people's decisions to abort have occurred in the context of excruciating trauma, conflict, pressures and/or challenges that my parents didn't have as part of their story, and carry deep empathy for them.

Two years after my birth, Mum was critically ill and unexpectedly pregnant again. An abortion was advised again but Mum and Dad wouldn't consider this as an option. Amidst the powerful mix of emotions that this raised, Mum opened a book randomly to a beautiful picture of a mother tenderly holding an infant in her arms, captioned something like 'each life, a precious gift'. This reinforced for Mum that they were making the right decision. As a lifesaving measure Mum's whole bowel was removed and an ileostomy performed. A few months later my sister Alison Muriel was born on 7th February 1962. Mum lived for more than fifty years after this, passing on at the age of 84.

Three generations: Lois, Ailsa and Ellie (Lois' daughter)

Conclusion

We don't know anyone whose life has not been interrupted by serious roadblocks along the way. For some young women a roadblock may come in the form of an unintended or unwanted pregnancy. What should be the most joyful realisation in the world can instead deliver an overwhelming sense of despair. It can also be the loneliest time in a woman's life. In the midst of the turmoil of emotions, the words of encouragement from the people closest to her can be absent. Advice and even pressure to abort can come from the father of the child, from her wider family circle and even friends. But ultimately, she is the one carrying a new life within her womb, and it is she who carries the responsibility for that child. And sadly, if she decides to have an abortion, it is she who primarily must bear the potentially devastating consequences for the rest of her life. Because every woman knows well that if nothing untoward happens to stop development, in a few short months she would be holding her baby in her arms.

There are many reasons why pressure, at times intense, is placed on a woman to submit to an abortion. But it is never the easy answer some would promote it as being. The decision to abort a child is always a tragedy. The slogan "My body, my choice" is shallow comfort because it also infers, "my fault". In a similar way to someone considering suicide, the decision to abort is made because it is believed there is no other way through this roadblock. There is no hope.

But there is always hope. The stories of these brave women should inspire each one of us to resolve that our first words to any newly pregnant woman should be, "That's wonderful! A beautiful life."

Amanda Brohier and Robyn Graham

Support Resources

Genesis Pregnancy Support Inc
Free Unplanned Pregnancy Counselling,
Post Abortion Counselling, and Material Assistance
Post Abortion Healing Retreats also available
Phone (08) 8352 4044
www.genesispregnancysupport.org.au

Birthline Pregnancy Support Inc
24 hour Counselling Hotline and Material Assistance
Phone 1300 655 156 or (08) 8331 1223
www.birthline.org.au

Abortion Grief Australia
Abortion Grief, Pregnancy Crisis and Men and Abortions
National Helpline 1300 887 066
www.abortiongrief.asn.au

Pregnancy Help Australia Ltd.
Information, resources and referrals regarding pregnancy
support or pregnancy loss
24hr National Helpline 1300 139 313
www.pregnancyhelpaustralia.org.au

Endorsements

"These stories are heart-rending. They provide further proof that abortion taints everything it touches: from the abortionists who lie to themselves, to the counsellors who lie to their patients, to the women who go on to lead lives marked by unimaginable grief. May these testimonies and those of the mothers who rejected abortion inspire many other parents to choose life for their children."

Kathy Clubb

"This book is a powerful testimony of many women from all backgrounds experiencing several common factors when making the decision to abort their unborn child. It shows how abortion can affect our mental health and cause many of us to live a life of shame and regret. As hard as it was to relive my story through reading others, I hope and pray this book will be a resource to those who are choosing to make a decision to abort their unborn child. Thank you for the privilege of reading *Beautiful Life.*"

Jenny

"I am so very grateful for the brave women who have shared their stories. I am also thankful for the women who have compassionately compiled them so that others might find a way out of the horrendous emotional trap in which abortion leaves so many women.

The shameful truth is that many thousands more stories could be written by so many other women whose pain is not recognised or validated, leaving them all alone in their misery and mental torture with no hope of help. They have suffered silently long enough.

As the CEO of a pregnancy support centre, who has counselled many, many women over the past twenty years, I can assure you from firsthand experience that the connection between abortion and mental health is real. Don't ever accept the cold, callous and insensitive statement to the contrary. The research is in! This book is a wonderful help in paving a way out of despair into hope and healing."

Juli Sharpe

Genesis Pregnancy Support Inc

"These stories are potent. Often sad and charged with emotion, yet powerful illustrations of truths that refuse to be suppressed. They point to an abortion culture that silences deep intuitions and keeps loved ones from saying what in their heart of hearts they know to be true. Far too many lies have been told.

Yet these stories are hopeful too. Hopeful that healing and restoration are gifts freely given. That wholeness after grief and despair is possible.

Hopeful too because they may help others choose life."

Dr Gregory K Pike

Director

Adelaide Centre for Bioethics and Culture

"In a secular world, there is nothing more sacred than the love between mother and baby. Where that love is violated by abortion, there is nothing more moving than stories like these told by women who felt they had no choice, panicked and pressured into an abortion they didn't want.

Rage at the selfishness of males who seek sex without responsibility and bully their partner to abort. Realise that our culture is now deeply brutalised, formally abandoning women and babies in law, enshrining abortion on demand, caring nothing for innocent babies or for the ensuing epidemic of mental and emotional harm to women. So what can be done? As always in dark times, the task is to light one candle.

As this book shows, many women would turn away from abortion if they heard just one kind word of support. The task is to ensure they get to hear that word of support, whether from a doctor, a counsellor or a friend. To see just one image of truth, whether on an ultrasound or a beautiful pro-life flyer. And if the abortion is in the past, to know that there is a path to forgiveness and hope.

Saving just one baby and mother from the deathly effects of abortion is the most beautiful task in the world. This small book of stories will help."

Dr David van Gend
Queensland secretary for the World Federation of Doctors
who Respect Human Life

www.ingramcontent.com/pod-product-compliance
Lightning Source LLC
Chambersburg PA
CBHW070930270326
41927CB00011B/2798

* 9 7 8 1 9 2 5 8 2 6 7 4 6 *